Rainy Day

Written by David Orme
Illustrated by Bethan Matthews

Collins Educational

When Becky woke up she jumped out of bed, had a big yawn, scratched her head,

opened her window, looked out and said...

"Oh bother the rain!"

So she…
got back into bed,
and went to sleep again.

When Becky woke up she jumped out of bed, had a big yawn,

scratched her head,
rubbed her eyes,
wiggled her toes,
found her hanky,
blew her nose,

opened her window, looked out and said...

"Oh bother the rain!"

So she...
got back into bed,
and went to sleep again.

When Becky woke up she jumped out of bed, had a big yawn, scratched her head, rubbed her eyes,

wiggled her toes,

found her hanky,
blew her nose,

patted her tummy and licked her lips,
put on her dressing gown, did up the zip,
opened her window, looked out and said...

"*Oh bother the rain!*"
So she...
got back into bed,
and went to sleep again.

When Becky woke up she jumped out of bed,
had a big yawn, scratched her head,
rubbed her eyes, wiggled her toes,
found her hanky, blew her nose,
patted her tummy and licked her lips,

put on her dressing gown, did up the zip,

found her slippers under the bed,

opened her window,
looked out and said...

"It's stopped raining!"

So she...
rubbed her eyes, wiggled her toes,
found her hanky, blew her nose,
patted her tummy and licked her lips,
took off her dressing gown (undoing the zip),
took off her slippers

and looked for her sock,

put on her vest and her summer frock,

jumped down the stairs,

opened the door,

ran into the garden,

and guess what she saw?

A great big black cloud just ready to pour!

"Oh bother the rain!
I'm going back to bed again!"